# Vegan Comfort Food Cookbook

*Favorite Plant-Based Recipes You'll Love*
*(2022 Guide for Beginners)*

## Hazel May

# CONTENTS

# Introduction: Vegan FAQs

# "You're vegan? What do you even eat?"

You've probably heard this question 101 times since making the ethical and sustainable decision to go vegan. "Umm... stuff that doesn't come from animals?" is most likely your response.

People are frequently taken aback by this, but the truth is that a lot of food is already vegan—and with a little imagination and the correct ingredients, you can vegan-ify practically anything else.

People frequently believe that being vegan is restrictive or a diet, however, this is not the case. Most vegans enjoy eating; they simply prioritize their ethics and principles when deciding what to eat.

If you're new to vegan cooking, you might have some questions, so read the introduction before diving into the delicious and simple recipes in this book for tips, tricks, and useful information.

"Where do you get your protein?"

This is yet another vexing subject that vegans are frequently asked. People act as though meat and dairy are the only protein sources on the planet!

In reality, most people in wealthy countries consume far too much protein. If you're new to the vegan diet, you should spend some time calculating protein and planning your meals to ensure you're receiving enough, but protein insufficiency is uncommon.

Amino acids are chemical substances that are involved in a wide range of bodily activities. Proteins are formed when amino acids join together in long chains. While our bodies can synthesize numerous amino acids on their own, there are nine forms that the human body cannot produce. This means that we must rely on our meals to meet these requirements.

Vegans should bear in mind that not all protein sources include all of the amino acids that they require. In truth, the majority do not. But don't worry: as long as you have all of these amino acids in one day, you should be good.

That implies you can't rely on just one or two kinds of protein per day. When eating vegan, a good rule of thumb is to include two types of protein in each meal. This may appear to be a hassle, but you'd be amazed at how many foods contain protein. You won't even think about getting adequate protein once you've gotten used to eating a vegan diet and creative cooking.

Find out how many grams of protein you should consume per day by consulting a dietitian or searching online. To make things easier, each recipe in this cookbook specifies the number of grams of protein in a serving.

If you're tired of answering the protein question, take a look at five popular vegan proteins, how to use them, and their nutritional benefits.

### Beans, black

Did you know that the darker the color of a bean, the higher the number of antioxidants it contains? Black beans are unquestionably a vegan staple. With 15 grams of protein and 15 grams of fiber per cooked cup, black beans are a terrific way to make a meal more substantial. This cookbook contains numerous dishes that incorporate this hearty bean, ranging from Mexican meals to brownies (yes, brownies).

### Walnuts

Vegans can also get protein from nuts and seeds. This nut, which is high in healthy fats and protein, is a terrific snack or complement to a meal to help you feel full. Crush walnuts and add them to sweets, pasta, or even pizza!

### Quinoa

Quinoa may be the vegan protein king. This seed (yes, quinoa is actually a seed, but it's served as a grain) was once consumed by Incan warriors and provided a full amino acid group. That implies you won't have to worry about combining proteins if you consume quinoa. Quinoa is delicious in salads, as a veggie burger, or with curry. Quinoa spaghetti is even available at your local health food store.

### Chickpeas

This adaptable bean can be used for more than just hummus (although hummus is a delicious vegan staple you should master). Chickpeas provide 14.5 grams of protein per cooked cup, as well as 11 grams of fiber, manganese, and folate, an important nutrient for women. Chickpeas are delicious in curries, salads, stews, and a variety of other dishes.

### Oats

There's no vegan breakfast quite like cinnamon and brown sugar oatmeal, and that's not even the best part about oats. Oats have been shown to help lower cholesterol, so if you turned vegan for your heart health (a wise decision), you should incorporate oats into your diet whenever possible. Gluten-free? Not to worry! Gluten-free oats and oat flour are widely available.

### Tofu

Tofu, made from soybeans, is a vegan favorite, yet most non-vegans dislike it. Why has tofu earned such a nasty rap? Who knows, but maybe your carnivorous pals may become tofu fans after trying the dishes in this book. No vegan diet is complete without tofu, which has only 178 calories per serving but 12 grams of protein. Bread, fry, bake, or combine it; the options are unlimited, so get creative with this protein-packed delight.

Buy GMO-free tofu since the health effects of eating genetically modified soybeans are unknown.

### Lentils

Lentils are a bean that appears in cuisines all across the world, from French to Indian, and frequently in this cookbook. Lentils, which contain 18 grams of protein per cooked cup, are an excellent complement to stews, vegetarian burgers, salads, and meat substitutes.

"Can you eat this?"

Yes, is a quick response to this question. As a vegan, you are theoretically allowed to eat anything; you simply choose not to. Whether you became a vegan for health, weight reduction, the environment, your love of animals, or all of the above, don't allow your lifestyle choice to limit you. Eating vegan may, with some practice and imagination, open new doors to culinary delights rather than close them.

"Is this really vegan?"

When dining at a vegan restaurant, you may find yourself asking this question. How do they make cuisine that is creamy, buttery, or cheesy without the use of dairy? Vegan hacks are the answer. Every vegan should be familiar with a few pantry basics. These essentials aid in recreating flavors that aren't typically associated with a plant-based diet.

Once you've mastered these components, your next dinner party will be greeted with a chorus of "Is this actually vegan?"

## Cashews

Cashews are a must-have in any vegan pantry. Soak them for a few hours in the water, then drain and combine with herbs and spices to make creamy dipping sauces, or with sugar and chocolate powder to make vegan ice cream. The high-protein options are nearly limitless. Does anyone for cashew "milk" shake?

## Yeast Nutritional

Because nutritional yeast has a cheesy flavor, it is the first choice of most vegans when it comes to cheese substitutes. With only 40 calories and 3 grams of protein per tablespoon, it's low in calories but high in protein. Most vegans simply cannot live without nutritional yeast, and shops are well aware of this; as a result, it is frequently fortified with vitamins that vegans commonly lack, such as vitamin B12. Why bother taking a multivitamin when you can have creamy, delicious vegan queso every day?

## Tahini

Tahini, like cashews and nutritional yeast, is an easy method to boost protein in a meal. It's also high in good fats. Tahini adds richness as well as a nutty taste to recipes, making it an excellent addition to curries and stir-fries. Tahini is also an excellent base for salad dressings and glazes. If you have a nut allergy, you can substitute tahini for nuts in a variety of dishes.

### Avocado

Another technique to add creaminess to recipes is to use avocado. Avocado is as healthy as it is delicious, with 13 grams of fiber and 4 grams of protein per serving. Avocados can be used to produce a delicious chocolate mousse or a decadent pasta sauce. To make a smoothie even creamier, add an avocado.

### Seeds of Flax

Flax seeds are a simple method to boost protein in any dish. Flax seeds are particularly abundant in omega fatty acids, which are essential for healthy skin. Simply toss some ground flax seeds into a smoothie for an instant energy boost. Doctors also recommend incorporating omega fatty acids into your diet during the winter, along with vitamin D, to combat the winter blues.

As if that weren't enough, these tiny seeds are also an excellent egg substitute. A tablespoon of ground flax seeds combined with a tablespoon of water yields a quick egg substitute that can be used in practically any recipe.

Because your body cannot absorb entire flax seeds, make sure you get ground flax seeds.

### Cauliflower

Cauliflower is a low-carbohydrate substitute for rice, potatoes, and even wheat, making it one of the most adaptable vegetables on the planet. Cauliflower is inexpensive in calories but abundant in vitamin C, making it a nutritional winner. Cauliflower becomes extremely creamy when boiled and combined, making it an ideal nutrient-dense cream substitute.

Replace heavy cream in soups and curries, or use it to make "cheese."

"Is being vegan expensive?"

Some specialty goods may be more expensive, but following a

vegan diet does not have to be a costly endeavor. Which is normally more expensive at the grocery store, meat or vegetables?

The greatest method to save money on a vegan diet is to shop at local farmers' markets and buy seasonal products. Buying from local farmers not only benefits your community but is also better for the environment because the product does not have to travel large distances.

**Check out this seasonal vegetable guide.**

Pomegranate, butternut squash, apples, pears, figs, sweet potatoes, arugula, beets, peppers, broccoli, celery, eggplant, cranberries, potatoes, lettuce, mushrooms, limes, pumpkins, green beans, and zucchini

Winter vegetables include beets, cabbage, oranges, Brussels sprouts, onions, clementines, kale, cauliflower, leeks, grapefruit, lemons, mandarin oranges, shallots, radishes, turnips, winter squash, and tangerines.

Asparagus, strawberries, cherries, rhubarb, kumquats, fava beans, apricots, chard, kiwis, new potatoes, peas, spinach, and spring onions

Avocados, peaches, cantaloupes, blackberries, mangos, bell peppers, lemongrass, chard, blueberries, okra, chickpeas, melons, collard greens, grapes, cucumbers, figs, plums, raspberries, spinach, watermelons, summer squash, nectarines

Organic produce is frequently more expensive than conventional produce, but it is better for the environment and your body because it is free of hazardous pesticides and other chemicals. That being said, eating entirely organic produce isn't always necessary.

Experts have created lists known as the Clean 15 and the Dirty Dozen. The Clean 15 are the 15 fruits and vegetables with the lowest pesticide levels and are thus safe to eat even if they are not organic. The Dirty Dozen are the 12 fruits and vegetables that contain the most chemicals. You should avoid eating these unless they are organic.

Corn, pineapple, cauliflower, honeydew, avocado, kiwi, onions, eggplant, cabbage, sweet peas, asparagus, papaya, mangos, cantaloupe, and grapefruit are among the Clean 15.

The infamous "Dirty Dozen"
Spinach, pears, strawberries, bell peppers, celery, nectarines, potatoes, cherries, apples, grapes, peaches, and tomatoes are all good choices.

"Is being vegan a lot of work?"

Being a vegan takes as much effort as you want it to. Many vegans regard their diet as a hobby as well as a way of life. Vegan cooking is enjoyable and creative, so if you see your vegan friends cooking for hours every day, it's generally because they enjoy preparing and eating beautiful, healthy meals, not because they have to.

Being a vegan can be a simple and low-maintenance lifestyle. Many of the dishes in this book don't even call for cooking and may be prepared in 10 minutes or less.

Being a vegan is a lot of fun now since there are so many delicious and nutritional options. As an added benefit, vegan food is typically lower in calories, allowing you to enjoy seemingly rich meals without jeopardizing your health or waistline.

Why would you eat meat or dairy when vegan food can be this healthy and delicious?

"Vegan Comfort Food?

Vegan food is generally healthier than traditional meals, but that doesn't mean it can't be just as decadent and cozy. Choosing a vegan lifestyle is about loving your body, animals, and the environment, not about making sacrifices or restrictions.

Cheese flavors can be delivered using creamed cashews and nutritional yeast. When you consider carob chips, which are seeds that taste and feel just like chocolate chips, you have a plethora of dessert options. Frozen bananas make excellent ice cream, and avocados are ideal for pudding. Are you feeling sluggish? Vegan pie crust, biscuit dough, and shredded cheese are all available at your local grocery store.

Going vegan is not as restrictive as carnivores believe! Sure, all of the dishes in this cookbook are healthier than their meat and dairy counterparts, but that doesn't mean you have to give up the flavor at all! Plus, these dishes, particularly the desserts, are a terrific way to get youngsters to eat their vegetables!

The recipes in this book range from really simple to slightly more complex, so you may choose something based on how ambitious you are and how much time you have. There are dinners for when you're sitting on the couch alone, family meals, holiday meals, and cocktail party food. There are also recipes from various countries as well as conventional American comfort cuisine!

There's no reason to give up all of your favorite foods and flavors when you go vegan. You can fulfill all of your eating fancies on a vegan diet with a little creativity and surprisingly little work.

So, be thankful for Mother Nature's bounty of tastes, and enjoy these decadent meals. You've earned it!

# BREAKFAST RECIPES

# PEANUT BUTTER CUP SMOOTHIE BOWL

Everyone remembers peanut butter cups from their childhood. This smoothie bowl delivers all the indulgence of a peanut butter cup, plus more protein! Add puffed rice cereal for some crunch.

*Yields: 2 servings – Prep. time: 10 min. – Cooking time: 0 min.*

## Ingredients

2 bananas, frozen
½ cup vegan milk
2 tablespoons peanut butter
2 tablespoons cocoa powder
2 tablespoons chia seeds
1 tablespoon maple syrup (if desired)

Optional Toppings: Banana, sliced
Puffed rice cereal
Carob chips
Vegan whipped cream

## Preparation

1. Add all ingredients to your blender and begin blending from low to high, adding more vegan milk as needed.
2. Serve in bowls with chosen toppings.

## Nutrition facts per serving

Calories 290, total fat 13 g, carbs 44 g,
Protein 8 g, sodium 96 mg

# BISCUITS AND GRAVY

Biscuits and gravy may be the ultimate Southern comfort food. This vegan version is just as delicious (if not more!) as the original. Eat your heart out, Paula Deen!

*Yields: 2 servings – Prep. time: 15 min. – Cooking time: 30 min.*

### Ingredients
For biscuits
2 cups all-purpose flour (plus extra for working surface)
1 cup vegan milk, unsweetened, plain
1 tablespoon baking powder
1 teaspoon salt
½ teaspoon baking soda
½ cup vegan butter, cold (plus extra for brushing on top)

For gravy
½ tablespoon onion powder 1 teaspoon thyme, dry
½ teaspoon garlic powder
1 cup vegetable broth¼ cup flour
2 tablespoons vegan butter
¼ cup red wine, dry

Optional
Vegan sausage

*Preparation*

1. Preheat oven to 450°F.

2. In a large bowl, mix together the dry ingredients for the biscuits.

3. Using a pastry cutter, cut in the cold vegan butter until the dough has become a coarse meal. The secret to Southern-style biscuits is using cold butter and working quickly so it does not melt. Quickly stir in the vegan milk, being careful not to overwork the dough so the butter doesn't melt.

4. Transfer the sticky dough to a well-floured surface. Form the dough into a 1-inch thick circular shape. Minimize your contact with the dough to prevent the butter from melting.

5. Use a biscuit or cookie cutter to cut out biscuits. Transfer the biscuits to a baking sheet and brush with butter. Make sure the biscuits are touching a little.

6. Bake until golden brown, up to 15 minutes.

7. While the biscuits are baking, mix one cup of vegetable broth with the onion and garlic powder. Bring the broth to a boil, then reduce to medium heat and stir in the flour and butter. Stir briskly while you pour in the flour so it does not become clumpy.

8. Allow to thicken for 10 minutes before adding the rest of the vegetable broth with the red wine and thyme. Cover and cook on the lowest setting for 15–20 minutes, stirring occasionally.

9. Once the gravy has reached your desired thickness, serve over the warm biscuits.

*Nutrition facts per serving*
Calories 332, total fat 19 g, carbs 35 g,
Protein 5 g, sodium 264 mg

# CINNAMON SWEET POTATO WAFFLES

There's nothing like warm, freshly made waffles in the morning. These waffles are extra special because they're gluten free, low carb, and loaded with nutrients—not to mention delicious!

*Yields: 2 servings – Prep. time: 15 min. – Cooking time: 10 min.*

### Ingredients
2 sweet potatoes, large
1 cup oats, old fashioned
2 flax eggs
2 cups vegan milk
2 tablespoons vegan butter
1 teaspoon salt
1 teaspoon baking powder
1 teaspoon cinnamon

Optional toppings: Banana
Maple syrup
Vegan butter

*Preparation*

**1.** Boil the sweet potatoes until very tender, about 15 minutes. (No need to peel them before boiling; the skins will peel off on their own once cooked.) Meanwhile, preheat the waffle iron.

**2.** In a blender or food processor, combine the cooked sweet potatoes and the rest of the ingredients. Blend until very smooth.

**3.** Spray the waffle iron with cooking spray and cook the waffles according to the manufacturer's instructions. This recipe makes two full waffles.

**4.** Serve with maple syrup and other toppings.

*Nutrition facts per serving*
Calories 455, total fat 18 g, carbs 64 g,
Protein 10 g, sodium 505 mg

# BREAKFAST GALETTE

If you've never made a pastry before, galettes are for you. These lazy pastries are a delicious kind of peasant food, so feel free to throw in whatever you have in the kitchen. Rolled oats or apples make for a nice addition.

*Yields: 6 servings – Prep. time: 15 min. – Cooking time: 50 min.*

### Ingredients
1 butternut squash, small
1 sheet vegan puff pastry (or make pastry dough from scratch)
¾ cup vegan butter, divided
2–4 tablespoons maple syrup
1 teaspoon cinnamon
1 teaspoon vanilla extract
Pinch of salt

Optional:
¼ teaspoon nutmeg
¼ teaspoon ginger
Marshmallows
Apple
Rolled oats
Walnuts
Vegan whipped cream

*Preparation*

1. Preheat the oven to 375°F.

2. Cut the butternut squash in half and scoop out the seeds. Roast both sides of the squash until tender. This should take about 30 minutes.

3. Once the butternut squash is tender, scoop it into a large bowl, discarding the skins. Mix in ¼ cup of the vegan butter, plus the cinnamon and other seasonings. You can also add some maple syrup if you favor a sweeter breakfast.

4. Roll out the puff pastry on a floured surface, then place it on a baking sheet. Fill the puff pastry with the butternut squash and roll the edges about 2 inches over the squash, leaving the center exposed. Your galette won't look perfect, but that's part of the charm.

5. Bake for 15–20 minutes.

6. While the galette is baking, melt the remaining butter in a pan on the stove at medium high heat. Allow the butter to slowly brown, but don't let it burn.

7. Once the butter is golden brown and has a nutty aroma, immediately remove it from the heat, pour into a bowl, and mix in vanilla, salt, and the desired amount of maple syrup.

8. Once the puff pastry is golden, remove from heat and cover with the brown butter glaze. Serve warm or cooled.

**Nutrition facts per serving**
Calories 301, total fat 24 g, carbs 20 g,
Protein 1 g, sodium 261 mg

# ULTIMATE BREAKFAST BURRITO

Breakfast burritos may just be the best breakfast comfort food. Stuff them full of your favorite goodies and prepare for a decadent but protein-packed breakfast. Next time someone asks you where you get your protein, serve them this burrito! Gluten-free? No problem— serve your breakfast burrito over home fries or quinoa.

*Yields: 6 servings – Prep. time: 15 min. – Cooking time: 50 min.*

### Ingredients
4 flour tortillas
3 potatoes, large, cubed
Vegan queso (see recipe in "Cheese" section)
1–2 bell peppers, diced
1 onion, diced
1 block tofu, crumbled
1 teaspoon turmeric
2 tablespoons nutritional yeast
2 avocados, peeled and sliced
1 tablespoon baking soda
Salt
1 teaspoon garlic powder (optional)
Dash of paprika (optional)

*Preparation*

1.  Preheat the oven to 375°F.

2.  Boil the diced potatoes with baking soda until very tender. (The alkalized water makes the outside of the potatoes mushy, which will equal crispier home fries after baking.)

3.  When the potatoes are tender, which should take 15–20 minutes, drain them and then toss them with salt, olive oil, bell pepper, onion, and your chosen spices. Bake in the oven until golden brown and crispy, about 45 minutes.

4.  While the potatoes are baking, crumble the tofu into a skillet. Sauté on medium high heat until the tofu begins to become golden, about 10 minutes.

5.  Add turmeric and nutritional yeast to make tofu scramble. Continue sautéing until you've reached your desired consistency.

6.  Pack as much tofu, home fries, avocado, and vegan queso as you can into your burrito, roll it up and serve warm.

**Nutrition facts per serving**
Calories 637, total fat 22 g, carbs 83 g,
Protein 29 g, sodium 261 mg

# SOUP RECIPES

## BROCCOLI CHEDDAR SOUP

Broccoli cheddar soup is an American classic! This creamy soup is guaranteed to warm you up on a cold day. Make ahead and freeze for an easy lunch anytime. With nutritional yeast and cashews, this soup is surprisingly filling.

*Yields: 4 servings – Prep. time: 15 min. – Cooking time: 50 min.*

### Ingredients
1 potato, large, peeled and diced
2 carrots, medium, peeled and chopped
2–3 cloves garlic, minced
1 onion, diced
4 cups vegetable broth
4 cups broccoli florets
1 cup vegan milk ½ cup cashews
¼ cup nutritional yeast
Hot sauce (to taste)
Salt and pepper (to taste)
Olive oil

*Preparation*

**1.** In a large pot, sauté diced onions with olive oil until translucent, about 5 minutes. Add garlic and continue to sauté until fragrant.

**2.** Add vegetable broth, cashews, and all veggies except for the broccoli. Bring to a boil, then reduce the heat and allow to simmer for 15–20 minutes, until the veggies are tender.

**3.** Use an immersion blender to blend the soup until smooth, then add the broccoli, vegan milk, hot sauce, and nutritional yeast. Feel free to add flour if you want a thicker soup. Bring to a boil, then reduce heat. Cook until the broccoli is tender, about 10 minutes.

**4.** Serve warm.

*Nutrition facts per serving*
Calories 246, total fat 8 g, carbs 32 g,
Protein 13 g, sodium 266 mg

# BUTTERNUT SQUASH SOUP

Butternut squash soup is the perfect way to capture the flavors of fall. Low in fat, but high in fiber and vitamin A, this soup is as nutritious as it is comforting!

*Yields: 2 servings – Prep. time: 15 min. – Cooking time: 50 min.*

### Ingredients

1 small butternut squash, peeled and cubed
½ onion, peeled and diced
2–3 cloves garlic, minced
2–3 cups vegetable broth
1 tablespoon olive oil
1 tablespoon curry powder (optional)
Salt and pepper (to taste)

### Preparation

1. Preheat the oven to 400°F.

2. Toss the onion, garlic, and butternut squash in olive oil and roast until the squash is tender, about 40 minutes.

3. Add the veggies to a large pot with vegetable broth and blend with an immersion blender. Add more liquid until you reach your desired consistency.

4. Cook on medium heat until heated through. Serve warm.

### Nutrition facts per serving

Calories 120, total fat <1 g, carbs 14 g,
Protein 1 g, sodium 110 mg

# VIETNAMESE PHO

Pho may seem simple, but it has a surprisingly nuanced flavor thanks to star anise and cinnamon. Plus it's a perfect light, healthy meal to eat when you're feeling under the weather.

*Yields: 4 servings — Prep. time: 10 min. — Cooking time: 20 min.*

### Ingredients
4 ounces rice noodles
6 cups vegetable broth
2 cups water
2 whole star anise
3 cloves
1 cinnamon stick
3 cloves garlic, minced
1 inch ginger, peeled and shredded
Soy sauce (to taste)

Optional toppings:
Sautéed mushrooms
Fried tofu
Thai basil
Lime wedges Bean sprouts Hot peppers
Fresh mint

*Preparation*

1. In a large pot, bring the water, broth, and spices to a boil, then reduce heat. Cover and simmer for about 20 minutes.

2. While the broth is simmering, cook the rice noodles according to package directions. Do not overcook.

3. Strain the broth, add soy sauce, and serve over rice noodles. Add desired toppings.

***Nutrition facts per serving***
Calories 130, total fat <1 g, carbs 26 g,
Protein 2 g, sodium 262 mg

# GNOCCHI TOMATO SOUP

Soft, fluffy gnocchi is like pasta, but better. Gnocchi amps classic tomato soup up to the level of gourmet comfort food while making for a super-filling meal.

*Yields: 4 servings – Prep. time: 10 min. – Cooking time: 45 min.*

### Ingredients
1 onion, small, diced
4–6 cloves garlic, minced 10 tomatoes, diced
2–3 cups vegetable broth
1 tablespoons tomato paste¼ cup fresh basil, torn
10 ounces gnocchi, fresh
1 tablespoon olive oil
Vegan Parmesan cheese (to taste)
Salt and pepper (to taste)

### Preparation
**1.** In a large pot, sauté diced onions over medium heat until tender, about 10 minutes. Then add the minced garlic and sauté until fragrant.

**2.** Add the tomatoes, basil, 2 cups of vegetable broth, salt, and pepper, and bring to a boil. Reduce heat and simmer until the tomatoes are tender, about 30 minutes.

**3.** Use an immersion blender to blend the soup.

**4.** Add the gnocchi and bring to a boil. Cook according to package directions. This should take about 3 minutes. You may need to add an additional cup of vegetable broth to cook the gnocchi.

**5.** Once the gnocchi is cooked, immediately remove from heat to prevent overcooking, top with vegan Parmesan, and serve warm.

***Nutrition facts per serving***
Calories 373, total fat 14 g, carbs 53 g,
Protein 17 g, sodium 559 mg

# CREAM OF MUSHROOM SOUP

In Eastern Europe, people forage for mushrooms, dry them, and use them to make delicious soup all year round. Even if you can't get mushrooms straight out of the dirt, this mushrooms soup is warm, healing, and totally satisfying.

*Yields: 4 servings – Prep. time: 10 min. – Cooking time: 45 min.*

### Ingredients
4–5 cups mushrooms, fresh, chopped
1 onion, small, diced
3 cloves garlic, minced 1 cup vegan milk
3 cups vegetable broth
½ cup cashews
2 tablespoons vegan butter (or olive oil)
1 tablespoon white wine, dry ½ teaspoon thyme, dry
Salt and pepper (to taste)

*Preparation*

**1.** Sauté the onions, mushrooms, and garlic together with the vegan butter on medium high heat until the onions are soft, about 7 minutes.

**2.** Add the vegetable broth, wine, milk, cashews, and seasoning. Bring to a boil, then reduce heat. Cook on medium low heat until you have reached your desired consistency, 30–45 minutes. Use an immersion blender to finish the soup off.

**3.** Serve warm and season with salt and pepper.

*Nutrition facts per serving*
Calories 195, total fat 13 g, carbs 14 g,
Protein 7 g, sodium 254 mg

# SPICY COCONUT SOUP

Loaded with spices like lemongrass and ginger, this soup is as tasty as it is healing. It's also the perfect way to add a powerful punch of flavor to any meal.

*Yields: 4 servings – Prep. time: 10 min. – Cooking time: 25 min.*

## *Ingredients*
1 12-ounce can coconut milk
2 cups vegetable broth
1 block tofu, cubed
2 carrots, grated
1 onion, diced
2–3 cloves garlic, diced
1 stalk lemongrass, cracked open
1 red bell pepper, sliced
1 lime, sliced in four
2 tablespoons Thai red curry paste (make sure it's vegan)
1 tablespoon ginger, fresh, peeled and minced
1 tablespoon sesame seed oil (or olive oil)

Optional toppings: Sriracha
Bean sprouts
Mushrooms

*Preparation*

1.  Sauté onion and carrots with oil in a large pot until the onion is translucent. Then add the ginger, garlic, and curry paste. Sauté until fragrant, about 1–2 more minutes.

2.  Add the broth, coconut milk, veggies, and tofu.

3.  Simmer on low heat for 15 minutes.

4.  Scoop out the lemongrass stalk and serve warm with lime slices.

*Nutrition facts per serving*
Calories 319, total fat 25 g, carbs 14 g,
Protein 14 g, sodium 255 mg

# SAUCE AND CONDIMENT RECIPES

# RANCH DRESSING

Creamy ranch dressing is classic American fare. Throw this delicious vegan version on a salad or use it as a veggie dip for a lazy, yet healthy snack.

*Yields: 25 servings – Prep. time: 5 min. – Cooking time: 0 min.*

### Ingredients
2 cups vegan mayonnaise
½ cup vegan milk, unflavored and unsweetened
1 teaspoon garlic powder
1 teaspoon onion powder
3 teaspoons fresh parsley, chopped
½ teaspoon paprika (optional)
Salt and pepper (to taste)

### Preparation
1. Mix all ingredients together in a large bowl, slowly adding milk until you've reached your desired consistency.
2. Store covered in the refrigerator and serve chilled.

### Nutrition facts per serving
Calories 27, total fat 1 g, carbs <1 g,
Protein <1 g, sodium 2 mg

# GINGER DRESSING

Ginger dressing is a great way to marinate tofu or dress up a salad. It also goes great on stir fries and sushi! This dressing is your ticket to Asian-flavored comfort food.

*Yields: 25 servings – Prep. time: 10 min. – Cooking time: 0 min.*

## *Ingredients*
¼ cup olive oil
⅓ cup rice vinegar
2 carrots, peeled and shredded
2 cloves garlic, minced
2½ tablespoons ginger, peeled and shredded
2 tablespoons sesame seed oil
2 tablespoons soy sauce (or tamari if gluten-free)
2 tablespoons maple syrup
1–2 tablespoons lime juice
1 tablespoon tahini (optional)

*Preparation*

1. Combine all ingredients in a blender or food processor. Blend until you have reached your desired consistency.

2. Store covered in refrigerator.

***Nutrition facts per serving***
Calories 45, total fat 3 g, carbs 3 g,
Protein <1 g, sodium 158 mg

# FRENCH ONION DIP

French onion dip is another comfort food classic. This vegan version is oh-so healthy and packed with protein thanks to cashews and nutritional yeast. Serve with veggie sticks to entice the little ones into eating veggies, or with ruffle chips on game day.

*Yields: 16 servings – Prep. time: 10 min. – Cooking time: 50 min.*

### Ingredients
1 large onion, sliced
1 cup cashews, soaked
3 tablespoons nutritional yeast
2 tablespoons vegan butter
1½ tablespoons apple cider vinegar
1 teaspoon garlic powder
1 pinch brown sugar (optional)
Salt and pepper (to taste)

*Preparation*

**1.** Coat the onions with butter and sauté on medium heat until they are caramelized to your satisfaction. You may add salt and sugar to the onions while they cook. This should take 30 minutes to an hour.

**2.** Once the onions are done, add half of them to a blender or food processor with the remaining ingredients. Blend until smooth. Add the rest of the onions, season with salt and pepper, and serve warm or cold.

*Nutrition facts per serving*
Calories 63, total fat 5 g, carbs 4 g,
Protein 2 g, sodium 39 mg

# CREAMY BUFFALO SAUCE

One of the things vegans report missing the most is Buffalo wings. But just because you don't eat meat doesn't mean you have to miss out. This Buffalo sauce is great over vegan chicken, cauliflower bites, in a wrap, or on a salad. Get creative with this sauce!

*Yields: 16 servings – Prep. time: 10 min. – Cooking time: 0 min.*

### Ingredients
1 cup cashews, soaked
1 cup hot sauce of choice
½ cup vegan butter
1½ tablespoons apple cider vinegar
1 tablespoon BBQ sauce
1 tablespoon paprika
½ tablespoon garlic powder

***Preparation***
1. Combine all ingredients in a blender and blend until smooth. Store in an airtight container in the refrigerator.

***Nutrition facts per serving***
Calories 45, total fat 4 g, carbs 1 g,
Protein <1 g, sodium 232 mg

# CHIPOTLE AIOLI

This recipe is *super* easy, but loaded with flavor. Creamy aioli adds a touch of gourmet to any sandwich, wrap, or burger. It's also a great dip for French fries!

*Yields: 16 servings – Prep. time: 10 min. – Cooking time: 0 min.*

### Ingredients
1 cup cashews, soaked
½ cup vegan milk, unsweetened
3 chipotle peppers in adobo sauce
1 tablespoon maple syrup
1 tablespoon lemon juice, fresh
2 cloves garlic
Salt (to taste)

### Preparation
1. Add all ingredients to a blender and pulse until smooth. Store covered in the refrigerator.

### Nutrition facts per serving
Calories 47, total fat 3 g, carbs 3 g,
Protein <1 g, sodium 41 mg

# VEGAN CHEESE RECIPES

# CAULIFLOWER ALFREDO SAUCE

Nothing is as soothing as cheesy pasta Alfredo. Think vegans can't enjoy? So wrong.

*Yields: 6 servings – Prep. time: 10 min. – Cooking time: 60 min.*

### Ingredients
1 head cauliflower
6 cloves garlic
½ cup vegan Parmesan
½ cup vegan milk, unsweetened
Salt and pepper to taste

### Preparation
1. Roast the cauliflower and garlic at 400°F until very tender, about 40 minutes.

2. Add all ingredients to a food processor and blend until smooth.

3. Serve over pasta topped with vegan Parmesan.

### Nutrition facts per serving
Calories 75, total fat 4 g, carbs 8 g,
Protein 5 g, sodium 107 mg

# PARMESAN CHEESE

Parmesan cheese is an easy way to add salty creaminess to a recipe. Luckily for herbivores everywhere, you can make vegan Parmesan cheese in just a few minutes.

*Yields: 16 servings – Prep. time: 10 min. – Cooking time: 0 min.*

### Ingredients
½ cup cashews, unsalted
½ teaspoon garlic powder
¼ cup nutritional yeast
½ teaspoon sea salt (optional)

### Preparation
1. Add all ingredients to a food processor and blend until you've reached your desired texture. The mixture should be dry, nutty, and cheesy, like Parmesan cheese.

### Nutrition facts per serving
Calories 60, total fat 4 g, carbs 3 g,
Protein 3 g, sodium 357 mg

# SPINACH ARTICHOKE DIP

Cheesy spinach artichoke dip is perfect for a dinner party, a girls' night, or just binging in front of the TV! With vegan cheese and plenty of veggies, there's no reason to feel guilty about this little indulgence.

*Yields: 10 servings – Prep. time: 10 min. – Cooking time: 15 min.*

### Ingredients
1 8-oz bag vegan mozzarella shreds
1–2 cups marinated artichoke hearts, chopped
3 cloves garlic, minced
½ cup vegan milk, unsweetened (or vegan cream cheese)
2–4 cups baby spinach, fresh ½ cup vegan Parmesan
¼ cup breadcrumbs (optional) 1 tablespoon olive oil
Salt and pepper (to taste)

*Preparation*

1.  Preheat oven to 400°F.

2.  In a pan, sauté the garlic over medium heat until fragrant, about 1 minute. Add the spinach and artichoke hearts and sauté until the spinach has wilted. Add salt and pepper, mozzarella, and vegan milk. Stir.

3.  Pour the mixture into a baking dish and top with vegan Parmesan and bread crumbs. Bake for 5–10 minutes, until the top has slightly browned.

4.  Serve warm with tortilla chips, bagel chips, crusty bread, or veggie sticks.

**Nutrition facts per serving**
Calories 102, total fat 4 g, carbs 12 g,
Protein 5 g, sodium 428 mg

# SWEET POTATO QUESO

Rich, creamy, spicy nacho cheese. Why eat dairy when you can create the same effect with just sweet potatoes and a few other ingredients? Perfect for game day dip, on a burger, or in a wrap. Not to mention nachos!

*Yields: 12 servings – Prep. time: 10 min. – Cooking time: 35 min.*

### *Ingredients*
2 cups sweet potatoes, whole, unpeeled
¼ cup nutritional yeast
1 tablespoon arrowroot powder
Hot sauce (to taste)
Jalapenos (to taste) 1 teaspoon salt
Water (as needed)

*Preparation*

1.  Steam the sweet potatoes for about 25–30 minutes.

2.  When they are tender, remove the skins and place the potatoes in the food processor with the rest of the ingredients.

3.  Blend together, adding water as needed. You should end up using about ¼ cup of water.

4.  Serve hot or cold.

***Nutrition facts per serving***
Calories 33, total fat 30 g, carbs 49 g,
Protein 13 g, sodium 532 mg

# ALMOND FETA

Feta cheese is tangy, creamy, and the perfect companion to Greek food. Add this "cheese" to a hummus platter, load it on top of a Greek burrito bowl, or throw it into a wrap. The possibilities are endless with this uber-healthy cheese replacement.

*Yields: 12 servings – Prep. time: 10 min. – Cooking time: 40 min.*

### Ingredients
1 cup almonds, soaked for 24 hours
¼ cup water
¼ cup lemon juice, fresh
2 tablespoons olive oil + extra for drizzling
1 teaspoon salt
1 garlic clove

*Preparation*

   **1.** Combine lemon juice, soaked almonds, water, olive oil, salt, and garlic in a blender or food processor and blend until smooth.

   **2.** Pour the mixture into a cheesecloth and squeeze out excess moisture. Chill in the cheesecloth overnight.

   **3.** Preheat oven to 200°F.

   **4.** Shape the feta into a block and bake for 40 minutes until the top is firm.

   **5.** Chill and serve drizzled with olive oil.

***Nutrition facts per serving***
Calories 78, total fat 7 g, carbs 2 g,
Protein 2 g, sodium 569 mg

# MAIN COURSE RECIPES

# CORN CASSEROLE

Corn casserole is perfect for the holidays, but unfortunately it's usually made with animal fat. Gross! This version is completely cruelty free. Take it with you to Thanksgiving, or make it anytime you need an easy, warm meal.

*Yields: 6 servings – Prep. time: 5 min. – Cooking time: 45 min.*

### Ingredients
2 cups corn kernels
1 14.75-ounce can cream style corn
1 8.5-ounce box corn muffin mix (make sure it's vegan)
1 cup vegan milk, unsweetened (or vegan sour cream)
¼ cup vegan butter
½ cup mushrooms (optional)

*Preparation*

1.   Preheat oven to 350°F.

2.   Mix all ingredients together in a large bowl. Pour the mixture into an oven-safe baking dish.

3.   Bake for 45 minutes, until the top is golden brown.

4.   Serve warm.

*Nutrition facts per serving*
Calories 282, total fat 12 g, carbs 41 g, Protein 5 g, sodium 623 mg

# FRIED "CHICKEN"

Fried chicken is another one of those dishes vegans report missing the most. Luckily, clever chefs have come up with a way to recreate the fried chicken flavor. Whether you use tofu, store-bought "chicken," or another meat replacement, you'll still get that signature crunch.

*Yields: 6 servings – Prep. time: 5 min. – Cooking time: 15 min.*

### Ingredients
1 pound vegan chicken, tofu, seitan, or other meat replacement
1 cup oil
1½ cups flour 3 tablespoons cornmeal
¼ cup nutritional yeast
1 teaspoon onion powder
1 teaspoon garlic powder
1 teaspoon paprika
½ teaspoon cumin
1½ tablespoons baking powder
1 teaspoon salt
2 tablespoons brown mustard, spicy
⅓ cup water

*Preparation*

1. In a large bowl, mix together the dry ingredients.

2. In another bowl, mix the mustard together with the water. Add ⅓ cup of the flour mixture to make a batter. Mix together.

3. Dip your chosen meat replacement in the wet mixture, then the dry mixture.

4. Fry on medium heat in a large skillet until golden brown. Serve warm immediately with dipping sauces or on a bun for a "chicken" sandwich!

**Nutrition facts per serving**
Calories 572, total fat 45 g, carbs 29 g,
Protein 17 g, sodium 1041 mg

# GENERAL TSO'S TOFU

Sometimes the comfort food you crave is Chinese takeout. Unfortunately, most Chinese restaurants aren't all that vegan friendly, but that definitely doesn't mean that you have to miss out on the flavors.

*Yields: 4 servings – Prep. time: 5 min. – Cooking time: 15 min.*

## Ingredients
1 block firm tofu, cubed
3 tablespoons sesame seed oil, divided
1 tablespoon cornstarch
1 tablespoon garlic, minced (2 cloves)
1 tablespoon ginger, minced
3 tablespoons maple syrup
1 tablespoon rice vinegar
3 scallions, diced
¼ cup soy sauce, low sodium (or tamari if gluten-free)

## Preparation
1. In a large skillet, lightly fry the tofu with sesame seed oil until golden brown. Remove the tofu and set it aside.

2. Mix together the remaining ingredients and pour into the skillet. Bring to medium high heat and add the tofu. Cook until the tofu is heated and the sauce has thickened. Serve warm with rice or steamed veggies.

## Nutrition facts per serving
Calories 345, total fat 23 g, carbs 18 g,
Protein 17 g, sodium 578 mg

# POT PIE

Pot pies are one of those perfect self-contained meals. With a crispy crust and creamy veggies, this pot pie is like a hug for your tummy. This recipe is only a guide; feel free to get creative or use whatever you have around the house.

*Yields: 4 servings – Prep. time: 5 min. – Cooking time: 15 min.*

### Ingredients
1 roll vegan biscuits
1 onion, diced
2 cloves garlic, minced
2 cups veggie broth
2 carrots, peeled and chopped
2 stalks celery, finely chopped
2 large potatoes, diced ½ cup corn, fresh
1 cup mushrooms, chopped
½ cup vegan milk, unsweetened
¼ cup flour
½ teaspoon sage
¾ teaspoon thyme 2 bay leaves
1 tablespoon olive oil
Salt and pepper (to taste)

*Preparation*

1. Preheat oven to 425°F.

2. Sauté garlic and onions over medium heat until the onions are tender, about 5–7 minutes.

3. Add the milk and vegetable broth, then slowly whisk in the flour. Add the remaining ingredients, except for the biscuits, and allow the mixture to simmer until it has thickened to a gravy, 10–15 minutes. You can add more flour if needed. Throw away the bay leaves.

4. Pour the mixture into an oven-safe dish and top with biscuits. If necessary, roll out the biscuits to cover the entire dish.

5. Bake for 15 minutes or until biscuits are golden brown. Serve warm.

*Nutrition facts per serving*
Calories 317, total fat 7 g, carbs 57 g,
Protein 8 g, sodium 354 mg

# MAC & CHEESE

Every kid loves mac & cheese, and any adult who says they don't is lying. Vegans are just like anybody else, except this recipe is free of cruelty and cholesterol.

*Yields: 4 servings – Prep. time: 5 min. – Cooking time: 15 min.*

### *Ingredients*
1 cup pasta, dry
1 cup cashews, soaked ¼ cup nutritional yeast
½ teaspoon garlic powder
¼–½ teaspoon chili powder
¼ teaspoon chipotle powder
¼–½ cup vegan Parmesan (optional)
Salt (to taste)

*Preparation*

    **1.** Cook pasta according to package directions.

    **2.** In a food processor or blender, combine the soaked cashews with nutritional yeast and seasoning and blend until creamy.

    **3.** Combine the "cheese" with the cooked pasta and stir together. You can add vegan butter or vegan milk if you want a smoother texture. Top with vegan Parmesan, if desired.

*Nutrition facts per serving*
Calories 400, total fat 15 g, carbs 54 g,
Protein 18 g, sodium 93 mg

**GRILLED CHEESE**

Serve this easy grilled cheese with a bowl of tomato soup for a comforting meal that tastes just like home. This grilled cheese calls for three different cheeses, but feel free to pick whichever kinds you like best.

*Yields: 4 servings – Prep. time: 0 min. – Cooking time: 10 min.*

***Ingredients***
4 slices sourdough bread, thick
2 slices vegan cheddar
2 slices vegan Swiss
2 slices vegan pepper jack
1 tablespoon vegan butter
¼ teaspoon garlic powder

Optional toppings:
Caramelized onions
Jalapeno slices
Chipotle aioli

*Preparation*

**1.** Melt butter in a pan over medium heat and mix in garlic powder.

**2.** Make a sandwich with the bread and cheese.

**3.** Toast the sandwich in the pan with butter on medium heat until golden on each side, about 10 minutes.

**4.** Serve warm.

***Nutrition facts per serving***
Calories 310, total fat 12 g, carbs 43 g,
Protein 7 g, sodium 628 mg

# LENTIL SLOPPY JOES

Sloppy Joes may be a campsite classic, but they are definitely not healthy! This version, however, is made with lentils, high in protein and iron, so you can feel good about serving up this delicious meal.

*Yields: 4 servings – Prep. time: 5 min. – Cooking time: 25 min.*

### Ingredients
1 cup lentils (green, brown, or red)
1 tablespoon olive oil
1 onion, diced
3 cloves garlic, minced
1 bell pepper, diced
3 tablespoons tomato paste
2 tablespoons maple syrup
1 tablespoon Worcestershire sauce (make sure it's vegan)
1–2 teaspoons chili powder
1 teaspoon paprika
Salt and pepper (to taste)
2 cups water (or broth)
4 hamburger buns

*Preparation*

1.  In a large pot, heat oil and sauté onions over medium heat until tender. Add garlic and sauté until fragrant.

2.  Add the lentils and water. Bring to boil, then reduce heat. Cook until lentils are tender and water has reduced, about 20 minutes. If there is a lot of excess water, drain the lentils.

3.  Add the rest of the ingredients and simmer for about 5 minutes until the sauce becomes thick.

4.  Serve warm on buns.

*Nutrition facts per serving*
Calories 340, total fat 2 g, carbs 65 g,
Protein 17 g, sodium 311 mg

# "TUNA" SALAD SANDWICH

Replace the "chicken of the sea" with chickpeas for all the flavor and none of the chemicals, cruelty, and environmental damage of fishing. Perfect for a picnic, BBQ, or lunch!

*Yields. 4 servings – Prep. time: 10 min. – Cooking time: 0 min.*

### Ingredients
1 15-ounce can chickpeas, rinsed and drain
½ cup red onion, diced
½ cup celery, diced
2 tablespoons tahini
1 tablespoon mustard
1 tablespoon maple syrup
¼ teaspoon dill, dry (optional) 8 slices of bread
Salt and pepper (to taste)

### Preparation
1. Mix all ingredients together in a bowl, then serve over bread or on a salad. Mixed greens, avocado, and tomato make for great toppings.

### Nutrition facts per serving
Calories 318, total fat 4 g, carbs 57 g, Protein 13 g, sodium 577 mg

# SUPER EASY CURRY

Fall is the season for all things pumpkin. Creamy, warm, and super filling, this curry is a great way to experiment with nutrient-dense pumpkin. It's the perfect meal when you want something warm and tasty but don't feel like cooking very much.

*Yields: servings 4 – Prep. time: 15 min. – Cooking time: 30 min.*

### *Ingredients*
1½ cups pumpkin, peeled and cubed
1 13.5-ounce can coconut milk
2 15.5-ounce cans chickpeas, rinsed and drained
¼ cup curry powder 1 cup cauliflower
1 clove garlic, minced
1 tablespoon ginger, minced
Water (as needed)
Salt

*Preparation*

1.  For this simple recipe, all you need to do is add chopped pumpkin and cauliflower to a pot with coconut milk, curry powder, and salt to taste. Some curry powders already have salt in them, so you may not need to add any at all.

2   Bring to a boil and then reduce to a simmer. You may need to add water as the pumpkin cooks and liquid evaporates.

3.  Once the pumpkin is cooked to your desired tenderness you can use an immersion blender to make a creamy base, or you can leave it chunky.

4.  Add chickpeas to the curry and allow to heat up.

5.  Serve warm with a grain, naan, or alone.

### *Nutrition facts per serving*
Calories 375, total fat 20 g, carbs 31 g,
Protein 10 g, sodium 1352 mg

## PORTOBELLO BURGERS

Portobello burgers are a healthy and super-easy addition to any summer grill-out!

*Yields: servings 4 – Prep. time: 15 min. – Cooking time: 10 min.*

### *Ingredients*
4 portobello mushrooms, de-stemmed
4 hamburger buns
1 tomato, sliced
1 avocado
1 tablespoon balsamic vinegar
1 tablespoon maple syrup
1 teaspoon dried oregano
½ teaspoon onion powder
½ teaspoon garlic powder
¼ cup olive oil
Salt and pepper (to taste)
Chipotle aioli (optional)

## Preparation

1.  Mix together the liquid ingredients with the dried herbs, then soak the mushrooms in the marinade for at least 15 minutes.

2.  Grill the portobello mushrooms for about 5 minutes on each side.

3.  Top with avocado and tomato and serve on a bun.

## Nutrition facts per serving

Calories 212, total fat 8 g, carbs 28 g,
Protein 5 g, sodium 354 mg

# SWEET POTATO ENCHILADAS

These enchiladas are so easy to make that they're literally the perfect solution when you're just too lazy to cook a full meal.

*Yields: servings 4 – Prep. time: 15 min. – Cooking time: 10 min.*

### Ingredients
1 15-ounce can black beans
1 cup enchilada sauce (red or verde)
1 sweet potato, peeled and cubed, boiled or roasted
1 cup vegan cheddar shreds (optional)
4 flour tortillas

### Preparation
1.  In an oven-safe dish, stuff the tortillas with the cooked black beans and sweet potato.

2.  Top everything with enchilada sauce and cheddar cheese.

3.  Bake until warm and cheese is melted, 10–15 minutes. Serve warm.

### Nutrition facts per serving
Calories 361, total fat 6 g, carbs 62 g,
Protein 14 g, sodium 1334 mg

# BUFFALO VEGGIE BITES

You may be craving Buffalo wings, but these veggie bites are just as good! They're also a clever way to trick kids into eating their veggies.

*Yields: servings 6 – Prep. time: 10 min. – Cooking time: 40 min.*

### Ingredients
1 head cauliflower
1 cup butternut squash, peeled and diced
2 carrots, peeled and chopped
2 cups flour
3 tablespoons cornmeal¼ cup nutritional yeast
1 teaspoon onion powder
1 teaspoon garlic powder
1 teaspoon paprika
½ teaspoon cumin1½ tablespoons baking powder
1 teaspoon salt
2 tablespoons brown mustard, spicy⅓ cup water
1 cup vegan Buffalo sauce (see recipe)

*Preparation*

1.  Preheat oven to 400°F.

2.  In a large bowl, mix together the dry ingredients.

3.  In another bowl, mix the mustard together with the water. Then add ⅓ cup of the flour mixture to make a batter. Mix together.

4.  Dip the veggie pieces in the wet batter, then the dry batter.

5.  Bake until golden brown and crispy, about 30–40 minutes.

*Nutrition facts per serving*
Calories 284, total fat 4 g, carbs 48 g,
Protein 12 g, sodium 50 mg

# LOADED NACHOS

These nachos are as indulgent as it gets! Luckily, they're loaded with healthy proteins and veggies too! Invite your friends over to pull these cheesy babies apart.

*Yields: servings 6 – Prep. time: 10 min. – Cooking time: 20 min.*

## Ingredients
2 cups vegan cheese (cheddar shreds, vegan queso, or both)
1 15-ounce can black beans
1 red pepper, sliced
1 red onion, diced
1 cup salsa
1 bag tortilla chips
1 tablespoon vegetable oil
2 avocados, sliced

## Preparation
1. Preheat oven to 350°F.
2. In a large pan, sauté the red pepper and onion on medium heat with oil until the red pepper is scorched, about 10 minutes. Add salsa and heat for a few more minutes until warm.
3. Lay the tortilla chips out on a baking sheet or pan and top with the veggies, beans, and cheese.
4. Bake until the cheese is melted, about 10 minutes. Serve hot topped with salsa and avocado.

## Nutrition facts per serving
Calories 605, total fat 32 g, carbs 68 g,
Protein 12 g, sodium 1095 mg

# BROWNED BUTTER PASTA

This brown butter pasta is oh so gourmet, and yet it's also a superlazy meal. Perfect for when you need protein but don't want to cook something complicated.

*Yields: servings 4 – Prep. time: 0 min. – Cooking time: 25 min.*

## Ingredients
1 cup pasta, dry
¼ cup vegan butter
¼ cup nutritional yeast
1–2 cloves garlic, minced
½ cup vegan Parmesan

## Preparation
1. Cook the pasta according to package directions. Drain and set aside when finished.

2. In the same pot, heat the butter over medium heat. Cook until it begins to brown (it will foam up first), then add garlic and continue sautéing until fragrant.

3. Mix in the nutritional yeast, then add the pasta and stir. Serve hot topped with vegan Parmesan.

## Nutrition facts per serving
Calories 400, total fat 17 g, carbs 49 g, Protein 16 g, sodium 228 mg

## "SHEEP'S" PIE

Shepherd's pie is as filling as it is comforting. Sheep's pie replaces the meat with lentils, making this a perfect meal for filling lunch leftovers.

*Yields: 6 servings – Prep time: 10 min. – Cooking time: 40 min.*

### Ingredients
1 cup green lentils, dry
1 onion, diced
1 carrot, peeled and diced
1 cup cauliflower florets ½ cup red wine
1 cup vegetable broth
1 teaspoon thyme
2 cloves garlic, minced
3 potatoes
½ cup non-dairy milk
¼ vegan butter
1 cup vegan cheddar shreds (optional)
Salt

*Preparation*

1. Preheat oven to 425°F.

2. Boil the potatoes for 30 minutes. Remove the skins and add non-dairy milk, vegan butter, and salt. Mash to desired consistency and set aside.

3. Sauté the onion and garlic in butter or olive oil until the onions are tender. Add the broth, wine, thyme, and lentils. Bring to a boil, then reduce to a simmer and cook for 30 minutes.

4. Add the veggies and cook for another 10 minutes, until the lentils are tender. If you would like a thicker veggie mix, add a few tablespoons of mashed potatoes at this point.

5. Pour the veggie-and-lentil mixture into an oven-safe dish and cover with mashed potatoes and vegan cheese, if desired. Bake for 15 minutes, or until the tops of the mashed potatoes are golden.

*Nutrition facts per serving*
Calories 272, total fat 8 g, carbs 38 g,
Protein 11 g, sodium 221 mg

# DRUNKEN NOODLES

Drunken noodles are an easy Thai classic that serve up the unique flavors of Thailand without that much work! Sub eggs for tofu for a protein-packed, cruelty-free meal.

*Yields: 4 servings – Prep. time: 10 min. – Cooking time: 15 min.*

### Ingredients
10 ounces rice noodles
1 12.3 ounce package firm tofu, crumbled
3 cloves garlic, minced
¼ cup soy sauce
½ lime, juiced
1 tablespoon maple syrup
1 tablespoon sriracha
2 tablespoons sesame oil, divided
1 onion, diced
1 carrot, shredded
1 red bell pepper, sliced
3 scallions, sliced

*Preparation*

1. Cook the rice noodles according to package directions. Drain and set aside.

2. In a skillet, heat one tablespoon of sesame seed oil and fry the scallions, garlic, onions, and crumbled tofu until the onions are tender, about 7 minutes.

3. Meanwhile, mix the soy sauce, sriracha, lime juice, and maple syrup in a bowl.

4. Add the remaining veggies, noodles, and sauce mixture to the tofu and continue to sauté until the peppers are tender and the sauce has absorbed, about 5 minutes or less.

5. Serve warm.

*Nutrition facts per serving*
Calories 486, total fat 13 g, carbs 68 g,
Protein 20 g, sodium 725 mg

# SPAGHETTI AND "MEATBALLS"

You can never go wrong with spaghetti and meatballs—unless, of course, you don't go cruelty free. No animals were harmed in the making of this delicious comfort food classic!

*Yields: 4 servings    Prep. time: 10 min. – Cooking time: 25 min.*

### Ingredients

8 ounces spaghetti, dry
2 cups spaghetti sauce
2 tablespoons tomato paste
1 eggplant, roasted
1 15-ounce can chickpeas, rinsed and drained
1 cup breadcrumbs
2 flax eggs
½ teaspoon garlic powder
1 teaspoon basil, dry

*Preparation*

1.  Preheat the oven to 375°F.

2.  Cook the pasta according to package directions, then set aside.

3.  In a food processor, pulse the seasoning, tomato paste, eggplant, and chickpeas. You do not want the mixture to be smooth; it should be a little bit chunky.

4.  Pour into a bowl and mix together with breadcrumbs and flax eggs.

5.  Roll into balls and place on a baking sheet. Bake until browned, about 25–30 minutes.

6.  Serve on top of pasta and spaghetti sauce.

*Nutrition facts per serving*
Calories 603, total fat 8 g, carbs 68 g,
Protein 22 g, sodium 1191 mg

# SIDE DISH RECIPES

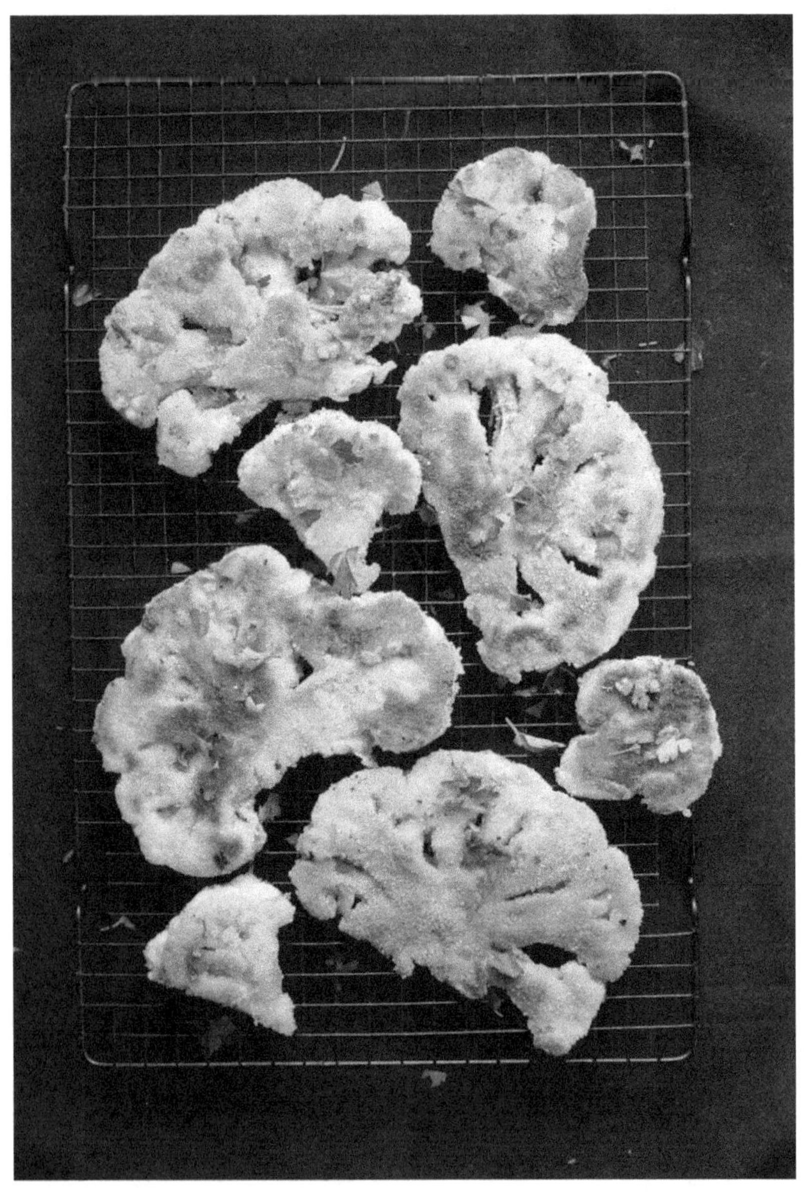

## SCALLOPED POTATOES

There's something about creamy potatoes in any form that really hits the spot. Although vegan, these are no exception.

*Yields: 4 servings – Prep. time: 10 min. – Cooking time: 25 min.*

### Ingredients
4 large potatoes, peeled and sliced
2 cups vegan milk, unsweetened
¼ cup vegan butter
¼ cup flour
Salt and pepper to taste

*Preparation*

1. Preheat the oven to 350°F.

2. Melt the butter over medium heat in a saucepan, then slowly add in the flour while whisking. Add the milk, salt, and pepper, and continue to whisk over heat until the sauce has thickened. This should only take a few minutes.

3. Put a few tablespoons of the milk-and-flour mixture in the bottom of an oven-safe dish, then layer potatoes on top and cover with the mixture.

4. Cover with aluminum foil and bake for 30 minutes.

5. Uncover and continue to bake for 45–60 minutes, until the potatoes are very tender and the top is browned.

*Nutrition facts per serving*
Calories 330, total fat 13 g, carbs 45 g,
Protein 9 g, sodium 183 mg

## MASHED POTATOES

At the end of the day, mashed potatoes will always be the king of comfort food. How many of us would rather sit down with a warm bowl of mashed potatoes than a dessert?

*Yields: 4 servings – Prep. time: 10 min. – Cooking time: 25 min.*

### Ingredients
2 large potatoes
1 cup vegan milk, unsweetened
1 tablespoon vegan butter
4 cloves garlic, roasted (optional)
Salt (to taste)

### Preparation
1. In a large pot, bring water and salt to boil. Add the potatoes whole. Reduce heat and boil for about 20 minutes until tender.

2. Remove the potatoes from the water and allow to cool for a few minutes, then remove the skins if you wish.

3. Add vegan milk, garlic, and butter and mash to your desired consistency.

4. Serve warm.

### Nutrition facts per serving
Calories 129, total fat 4 g, carbs 20 g,
Protein 4 g, sodium 65 mg

# FALAFEL

The crispy delight is the go-to comfort snack for many Middle Easterners. Because it's high in protein, it's now become a favorite for vegans as well!

*Yields: 6 servings – Prep. time: 2 hours – Cooking time: 20 min.*

### *Ingredients*
1 15-ounce can chickpeas, drained and rinsed
¼ cup parsley, fresh 2 tablespoons flour
¼ cup breadcrumbs
4 cloves garlic, minced
1 teaspoon cumin
2 tablespoons vegetable oil
Salt and pepper to taste

*Preparation*

1. Put all ingredients, except breadcrumbs, in the food processor and mix/chop until you have a chunky dough that holds together.

2. Pour into a bowl, cover and refrigerate for a few hours to help it hold together.

3. Mix in the breadcrumbs, then form into balls.

4. Coat a pan with vegetable oil and fry the falafel balls until brown and crispy. This should take about 5 minutes for each falafel ball.

5. Serve hot or cold.

*Nutrition facts per serving*
Calories 115, total fat 2 g, carbs 19 g,
Protein 5 g, sodium 65 mg

# CHILI CHEESE FRIES

With this recipe, you don't have to go to a carnival to get this classic binge-worthy food. Make these for your friends after a rough week or on game day!

*Yields: 6 servings – Prep. time: 5 min. – Cooking time: 20 min.*

### *Ingredients*
1 cup vegan queso (or cheddar shreds)
1 32-ounces bag frozen French fries
1 15-ounce can crushed tomatoes
2 tablespoons tomato paste
1 15-ounce can chili beans
1 tablespoon maple syrup
1 teaspoon paprika
½ teaspoon chili powder
½ teaspoon onion powder
½ teaspoon garlic powder

*Preparation*

**1.** Preheat oven and cook the French fries according to package instructions.

**2.** In a large pot, combine all ingredients except for the French fries and queso. Simmer the ingredients together until the sauce thickens, 5–10 minutes.

**3.** Remove fries from the oven and cover in vegan cheese and chili. Put back in the oven and bake for 5–10 more minutes.

**4.** Serve hot and enjoy.

***Nutrition facts per serving***
Calories 312, total fat 7 g, carbs 56 g,
Protein 12 g, sodium 1175 mg

# SWEET POTATO CASSEROLE

Sweet potato casserole is a delicious holiday treat, but it's rarely vegan. Sub vegan butter and marshmallows and there's no reason everyone can't enjoy this totally delicious side dish. Oh, and it's gluten-free and sugar-free. Yes!

*Yields: 6 servings – Prep. time: 5 min. – Cooking time: 45 min.*

### *Ingredients*
3 sweet potatoes, large
¼ cup vegan butter
¾ cup vegan milk, unsweetened
¼ cup maple syrup
1 teaspoon cinnamon
1 teaspoon vanilla extract
Salt (to taste)
Vegan marshmallows (optional)

*Preparation*

1. Preheat oven to 350°F.

2. Boil sweet potatoes whole for 15–20 minutes until tender. Remove from water and allow to cool before removing the skins.

3. Mix the potatoes together with the remaining ingredients and pour into an oven-safe dish. Top with more cinnamon or marshmallows if desired.

4. Bake until thoroughly warm and the marshmallows are melted, about 20 minutes. Serve warm.

**Nutrition facts per serving**
Calories 167, total fat 8 g, carbs 22 g,
Protein 2 g, sodium 233 mg

# DESSERT RECIPES

# MONKEY BREAD

You probably tried your hand at making monkey bread growing up. It's so easy, but packed with flavor. Next time you need a lazy, but next-level-delicious dessert, try this recipe.

*Yields: 10 servings – Prep. time: 15 min. – Cooking time: 30 min.*

### Ingredients

1 roll vegan biscuits, torn into pieces
½ cup vegan butter, melted
½ cup brown sugar, unpacked 1 tablespoon cinnamon
¼ cup cranberries (optional)

### Preparation

1. Preheat oven to 350°F.

2. Mix the brown sugar and cinnamon together in a bowl. Melt the butter in a separate bowl. Tear the biscuits into pieces.

3. Dip the biscuit pieces in butter and then in the sugar mixture until all the pieces are coated. Place in a baking dish, ideally a mini Bundt cake pan. Pour remaining butter over the biscuits. Gently push cranberries into the dough, if desired

**4.** Bake for 30 minutes, or according to package directions, then serve warm.

### *Nutrition facts per serving*
Calories 231, total fat 13 g, carbs 27 g,
Protein 3 g, sodium 250 mg

# SUPER EASY CHOCOLATE CHIP COOKIES

As many gourmet desserts as there are on the market, you really can't beat chocolate chip cookies. Homey, gooey, and oh so satisfying, no one will even know these are vegan. Sub gluten-free oat flour for your gluten-intolerant friends.

*Yields: 12 servings – Prep. time: 10 min. – Cooking time: 10 min.*

### Ingredients
1 cup flour
1 cup carob chips
1 cup brown sugar, unpacked
1 teaspoon vanilla extract
1 teaspoon baking powder
½ cup vegan butter, softened (or coconut oil)
½ teaspoon salt
1 flax egg

*Preparation*

1. Preheat oven to 350°F.

2. Mix all ingredients together until thick and creamy. Resist the urge to eat raw (or don't!).

3. Dollop the dough out into 1-inch balls. Bake at 350°F until golden brown, about 10 minutes.

4. Serve warm or allow to cool.

*Nutrition facts per serving*
Calories 304, total fat 19 g, carbs 34 g,
Protein 1 g, sodium 400 mg

## BLACK BEAN BROWNIES

These brownies are super decadent and yet oh so healthy. Made from black beans, these babies are protein packed and filling. Add these to the kids' lunch to keep them full all day, or add nuts for a surprisingly healthy and filling breakfast.

*Yields: 9 servings – Prep. time: 10 min. – Cooking time: 6 hours*

### Ingredients
1 15-ounce can black beans, sodium free, drained and rinsed
**1** cup vegan milk
½ cup oat flour
**2** flax eggs
¼-½ cup cocoa powder
½ cup maple syrup
¼ cup vegan butter (or coconut oil)
2 teaspoons vanilla extract
1 teaspoon baking soda

*Preparation*

**1.**   Add all the ingredients except the vegan milk to a food processor or blender. Slowly add the milk while blending until completely smooth. You may not need to use all of the milk.

**2.**   Preheat oven to 350°F.

**3.**   Pour the mixture into an oven-safe square pan, then bake for 15 to 20 minutes. Use a toothpick to test doneness.

## *Nutrition facts per serving*

Calories 230, total fat 12 g, carbs 28 g,
Protein 6 g, sodium 552 mg

# CHOCOLATE DIRT CUPS

Bet you didn't know this one could be made vegan. All of the smooth, chocolaty goodness—none of the cruelty or guilt. This is why being vegan is win-win-win.

*Yields: 9 servings – Prep. time: 10 min. – Cooking time: 6 hours*

### *Ingredients*
2 avocados
½ cup raw cocoa powder
¼-½ cup maple syrup (or agave nectar)
¼ cup vegan milk (as needed)
1 teaspoon vanilla extract
8 Oreo cookies, crushed
1 bag vegan gummy worms

*Preparation*

**1.** Combine the cocoa, avocados, vanilla, and sweetener in a food processor. Blend until smooth, adding vegan milk as needed.

**2.** Chill the pudding for about 30 minutes to 1 hour.

**3.** Line the bottom of 4 cups with crushed Oreos and gummy worms.

**4.** Pour the pudding into the cups and top with more crushed Oreos and gummy worms.

*Nutrition facts per serving*
Calories 230, total fat 12 g, carbs 28 g,
Protein 6 g, sodium 552 mg

# THE WORLD'S EASIEST FUDGE

Creamy fudge may remind you of summers at the boardwalk. Making fudge is usually pretty labor intensive, but this version could not be easier. Plus, with peanut butter, it's an easy way to get some extra protein into a meal. Be sure to share with gluten-intolerant friends!

*Yields: 24 servings – Prep. time: 30 min. – Cooking time: 0 min.*

## Ingredients
1 cup peanut butter
½ cup vegan butter (or coconut oil)
2–4 tablespoons maple syrup (to taste)
1 teaspoon vanilla extract Salt (to taste)
Pinch cinnamon (optional)

## Preparation
1. Blend all ingredients together in the food processor. Pour into a freezer-safe dish and freeze until firm, 15–20 minutes.

## Nutrition facts per serving
Calories 77, total fat 6 g, carbs 4 g,
Protein 2 g, sodium 56 mg

# CHOCOLATE S'MORES NICE CREAM

Marshmallows are hardly ever vegan, meaning you've probably missed out on a lot of campfire s'mores! Never worry, this nice cream is an easy way to get the same flavors!

*Yields: 4 servings – Prep. time: 10 min. – Cooking time: 0 min.*

## *Ingredients*

2 bananas, sliced, ripe, frozen ¼ cup cocoa powder
¼ cup vegan marshmallow fluff
Vegan marshmallows
4 vegan graham crackers
Vegan milk (as needed)

## *Preparation*

1. Add bananas and cocoa powder to your food processor (preferred) or blender if you do not have a food processor. Blend on high, adding vegan milk a little at a time until you reach your desired consistency.

2. Pour into a bowl and mix in vegan marshmallow fluff, then top with crumbled graham crackers and marshmallows.

3. Serve cold for dessert.

## *Nutrition facts per serving*

Calories 219, total fat 2.6 g, carbs 47 g,
Protein 4 g, sodium 76 mg

# MINT CHOCOLATE CHIP NICE CREAM

"Nice" cream is an easy way to "veganize" ice cream. Not only is this ice cream super healthy and creamy, it's ready in just a few minutes, unlike traditional ice cream! Eat this nice cream for dessert, or even for breakfast. It's also a great way to use overripe bananas.

*Yields: 2 servings – Prep. time: 10 min. – Cooking time: 0 min.*

## Ingredients
2 bananas, sliced, ripe, frozen ¼ teaspoon mint extract
Vanilla nut milk (as needed)
Handful carob chips

## Preparation
1. Add bananas and mint extract to your food processor (preferred) or blender if you do not have a food processor. Blend on high, adding nut milk a little at a time until you reach your desired consistency.
2. Mix in carob chips and serve immediately.

## Nutrition facts per serving
Calories 239, total fat 7 g, carbs 49 g,
Protein 1 g, sodium 15 mg

# COOKING CONVERSION CHARTS

## 1. Measuring Equivalent Chart

| Type | Imperial | Imperial | Metric |
|---|---|---|---|
| Weight | 1 dry ounce | | 28g |
| | 1 pound | 16 dry ounces | 0.45 kg |
| Volume | 1 teaspoon | | 5 ml |
| | 1 dessert spoon | 2 teaspoons | 10 ml |
| | 1 tablespoon | 3 teaspoons | 15 ml |
| | 1 Australian tablespoon | 4 teaspoons | 20 ml |
| | 1 fluid ounce | 2 tablespoons | 30 ml |
| | 1 cup | 16 tablespoons | 240 ml |
| | 1 cup | 8 fluid ounces | 240 ml |
| | 1 pint | 2 cups | 470 ml |
| | 1 quart | 2 pints | 0.95 l |
| | 1 gallon | 4 quarts | 3.8 l |
| Length | 1 inch | | 2.54 cm |

* Numbers are rounded to the closest equivalent

## 2. Oven Temperature Equivalent Chart

| Fahrenheit (°F) | Celsius (°C) | Gas Mark |
| --- | --- | --- |
| 220 | 100 | |
| 225 | 110 | 1/4 |
| 250 | 120 | 1/2 |
| 275 | 140 | 1 |
| 300 | 150 | 2 |
| 325 | 160 | 3 |
| 350 | 180 | 4 |
| 375 | 190 | 5 |
| 400 | 200 | 6 |
| 425 | 220 | 7 |
| 450 | 230 | 8 |
| 475 | 250 | 9 |
| 500 | 260 | |

*   Celsius (°C) = T (°F)-32] * 5/9
**  Fahrenheit (°F) = T (°C) * 9/5 + 32
*** Numbers are rounded to the closest equivalent